Logic

←A FIRST BOOK→

LOGIC

by Vicki Cobb

illustrated by Ellie Haines

FRANKLIN WATTS
London · New York

Franklin Watts Ltd
18 Grosvenor Street
London, W.1.

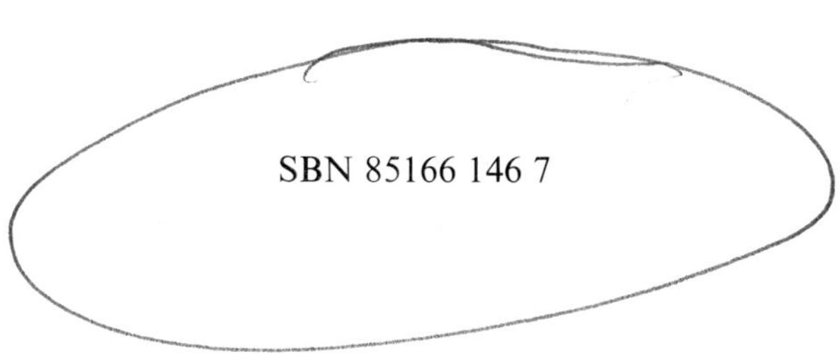

SBN 85166 146 7

Contents

Logic

About Being Reasonable

Anthropologists, who are concerned with the study of man, like to talk about the chief differences that make men superior to apes. For instance, apes use four feet for locomotion; man needs only two. That fact, anthropologists say, has encouraged the development of skills performed by man's hands. The hand of a man, with a thumb opposite to all the other fingers, can be trained to do things like play a violin or write with a pencil.

But the most outstanding accomplishment of man is the development of language. Language means that men can talk to each other about the problems of everyday life, even when they are not actually faced with these problems. (Animals have to teach each other by example.) Language means that the knowledge gained through the experience of one man can be shared with others to everyone's advantage. Language means that men

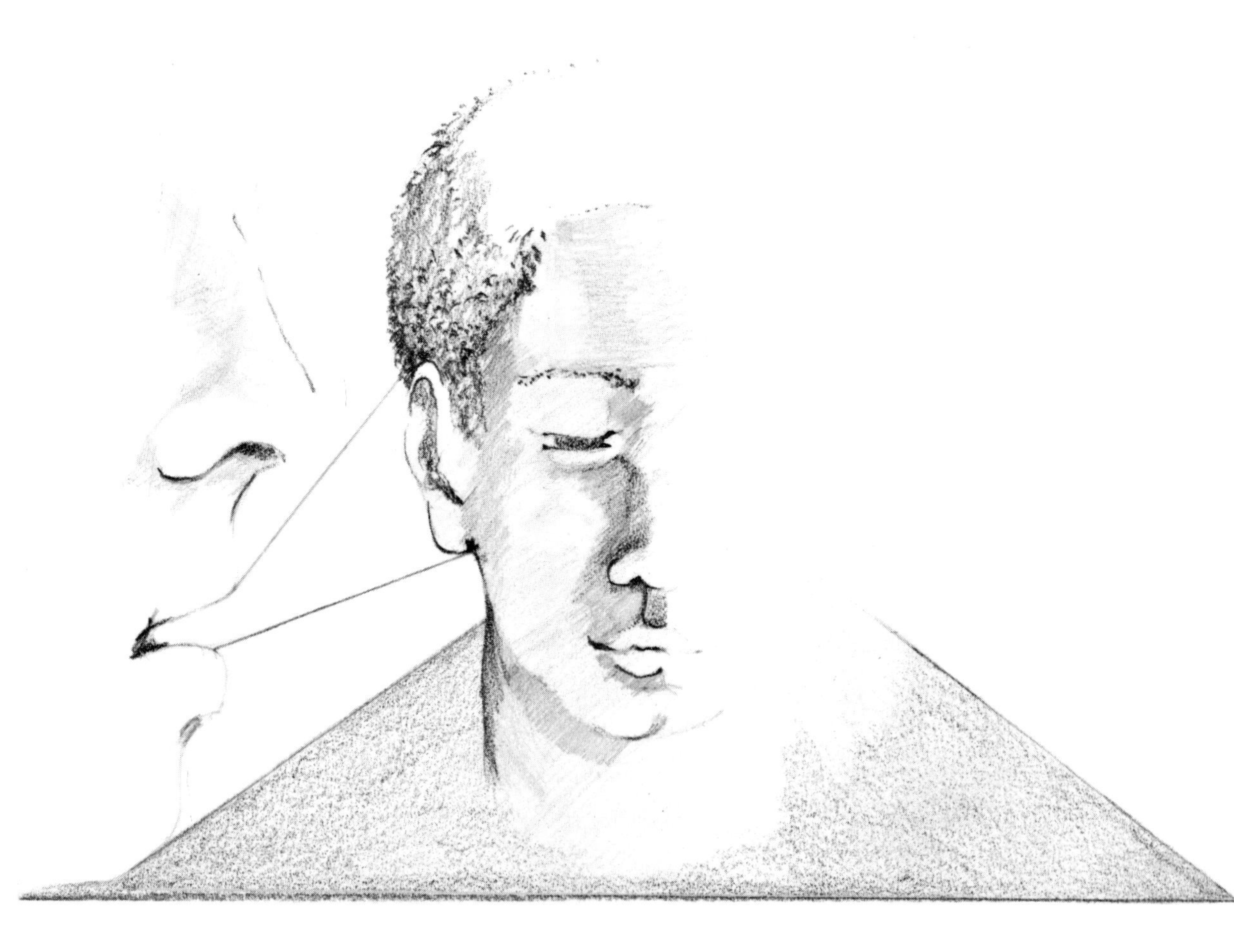

can disagree and can attempt to convince others of their own opinions without having to use violence. It is this last ability of man that brings us to the subject matter of this book.

People disagree. That is, they have different opinions. And very often when they disagree about something, they discuss it. The purpose of such a discussion is to make the other person change his mind and "come around" to the speaker's way of thinking. If you have ever overheard this type of discussion, you might have noticed such comments as, "You are not being reasonable" or "I'm not following your train of thought" or "You are not making sense." These comments indicate that a reasonable (or logical) argument is more likely to be convincing than one that does not "make sense."

You know this to be true yourself. Suppose, for example, you want to convince your parents that they do not need to tell you to do your homework; you are able to decide for yourself when to do it.

You could say to them: "I should be able to decide when to do my homework because I am thirteen years old. None of my friends' parents tell them when to do homework, and it would make me happier if you would leave me alone."

Or you could say: "I should be allowed to decide when my homework must be done because I am in a better position than you to arrange my schedule. I know better than you how much work has been assigned to me and how much time I need. Besides, it is a chance to let me show you how responsible I can be."

In both of the above examples you have presented a series of statements which someone who studies logic calls an *argument*.

Logicians define an argument as a conclusion that follows sup-porting statements, which are called *premises*.

(4)

In the two arguments on page 3, the conclusion is "I should be allowed to decide when my homework should be done."

In the first argument the premises are:

1. I am thirteen years old.
2. None of my friends' parents tell them when to do homework.
3. It would make me happier if you left me alone.

In the second argument the premises are:

1. I am in a better position than you to arrange my schedule.
2. I know how much work has been assigned and how much time I need.
3. It is a chance to let me show you how responsible I can be.

Logic is a system for distinguishing correct arguments from incorrect arguments. In a correct argument, you are able to predict the conclusion from the premises. Of the two arguments presented above, which one seems correct to you? Which premises are more directly concerned with the conclusion, "I should be able to decide when my homework should be done"? In this case, the second argument is correct. Yet, you can probably see that the first argument could convince some parents, especially if it is said with great emotion.

People use incorrect arguments more often than you would probably suspect. Incorrect arguments can be dangerous because they can be very persuasive despite the errors in reasoning. These arguments are called *fallacies* (from a Latin word meaning "to deceive"). Some of them are very common.

Common Everyday Fallacies

In a free society, such as in our country, a great many people try to get their opinions accepted. Parents want children to think they are right; politicians debate to convince the public to vote for them; businessmen advertise to convince consumers to buy their products; teachers lecture about how arguments from the past still apply today; and you, as a son or daughter, citizen, consumer, and student, must decide what to believe.

As you may know, very often this is not an easy job. First of all, there is the question of truth. Many arguments may be based on false premises. When you know that the premises are false it is easy to reject the argument. Surprising as it may seem, however, the truth or falsehood of premises is not the subject of logic. This is because many times we do not (or cannot) know if the premises are true or false. In fact, many arguments are fallacies even though they contain only premises that we know are true. These fallacies are dangerous because the truth of the premises is obvious, and people may be persuaded for the wrong reasons. Many of these fallacies are convincing because they take advantage of people's prejudices and emotions. One important skill in judging arguments is being able to recognize some of the more common fallacies so that they will not be able to convince you.

The Unrelated Conclusion

Many arguments are concluded with a statement that has little or no connection with the premises. This is perhaps the most frequent fallacy, and it may take many forms. You are probably very familiar with it although you may not have been aware of how such arguments are incorrect.

As an example, let us take the case of a father who tries to convince his son to become a football player. The father reasons, "Son, you could be a great football player because when I was your age I was a great forward."

The conclusion that the son could be a great football player has nothing to do with the kind of football player the father was. Football playing is learned, not inherited. What *is* related to the son becoming a football player is his own ability to learn the skills needed to play the game. (The father can *help* his son to be

a football player if he helps to teach him these skills.) The kind of argument used by the father in this example is often used by parents who have the mistaken idea that their children are just the way they, the parents, were when they were growing up. Conclusions about what children are able to do should be based on the abilities and interests of the children, not on those of the parents.

This fallacy of the unrelated conclusion also appears in discussions of national interest. There has been a great deal of discussion about how to end the war in Vietnam. One group argues for a military victory. Another group wants a withdrawal of United States forces. Some politicians in the middle look at both sides and conclude, "No one wants war." This conclusion is unrelated because wanting or not wanting war has nothing to do with arguments about how to end the war. The arguments offered for solving any national problem are usually very complicated, and you should be suspicious of quick and easy conclusions with which everyone can agree.

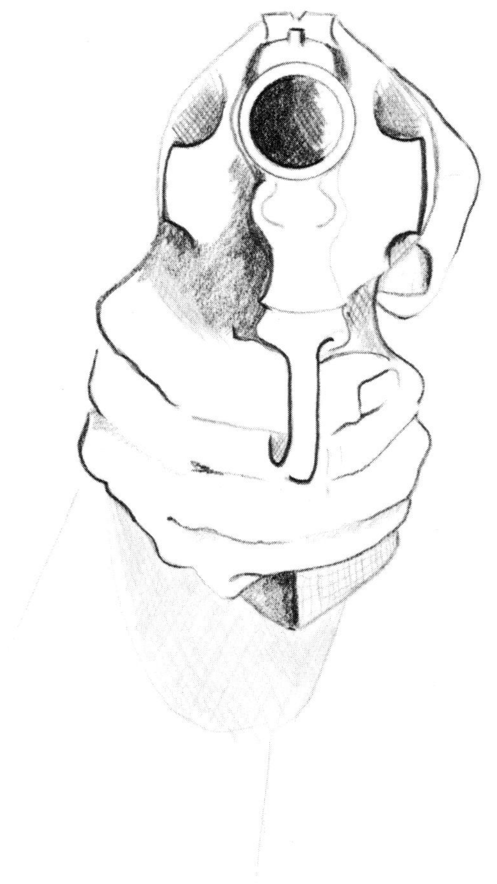

Might Makes Right

The gangster pointing a gun has very little trouble getting his victim to comply with what he says. What the gunman is saying, in effect, is, "Do what I say [agree with my conclusion] because I

Bill of
Rights

hold a gun." The use of force, or the threat of force, is not related to the actual reasons that the gangster has for wanting a person to do as he says. The gangster knows that his victim would not agree to do as he asks if he told him his premises. Do you think many people would give away their money because a man came up and said, "Give me your money because I have no job and I have to buy groceries and pay the rent"? Any use of force to get a conclusion accepted is a fallacy that can be summed up as "might makes right."

However, there are many examples of this fallacy that are not as obvious. The place of black people in the United States has been determined by the political and economic power of the white community. The black citizen can argue logically that under the law certain rights are guaranteed to him, such as the right to live wherever he can afford the rent, the right to work at any job for which he has the ability and training, and the right to have a fair trial. Yet, many times he cannot exercise these rights because of the power of some white people who will not rent to him, or hire him, or be unprejudiced jurists. And on the international level, too, many diplomatic discussions between nations are influenced by the military power of each country involved.

A Case of Name-Calling

Some people have a difficult time admitting they are wrong. If they become convinced that they will not be able to win an argument on the premises they have stated, they try to destroy their opponent's argument by calling him names. They think that discrediting their opponent will discredit their opponent's argument. They hope that this will convince onlookers that their own reasoning is correct.

Perhaps the most extreme form of this fallacy occurs during an election year in the form of political mudslinging. Politicians attempt to prove that their opponents are not qualified to hold public office and to use as "proof" all aspects of their opponents' lives and personalities, including those that have nothing to do with the office they are running for. The argument might be made that their opponents are not qualified for the job because of reli-

gion or because they never served in the armed forces. This fallacy
is also a form of the fallacy of the unrelated conclusion.

Name-calling, as a method of attacking an opponent, is usually
less obvious than political mudslinging. For example, a lawyer
might want to discredit the testimony of a doctor testifying in a
trial. A clever lawyer knows that he cannot come right out and
say that he thinks this doctor is incompetent. So, he might ask
the doctor a series of questions like these:

Lawyer: "Did you have a patient named Rufus Smith?"
Doctor: "I did."
Lawyer: "Where is he now?"
Doctor: "He is dead."
Lawyer: Oh, that's too bad. Did you also have a patient named
    Peter Jones?"
Doctor: "Yes."
Lawyer: "And is he dead, too?"
Doctor: "Yes."

The lawyer might continue naming others among the doctor's
patients who died. In this manner, the lawyer is trying to show
the jury that the doctor is not competent because so many of his
patients died. You can see that this is a fallacy because the lawyer
has not shown that the deaths of these patients were due to the
mistakes of the doctor.

Prove It Isn't So

If you ever want to change the course of someone who is building a case, choose a good moment to ask the simple question, "How do you know?" You might be amazed at the number of people who are unprepared to answer that question and who have been "talking off the top of their heads." They stumble and stammer out a reply such as, "Well, everyone knows that" or "I read it somewhere" or "What kind of question is that? Of course it's true." And you can be certain from the manner of their reply that they are not really sure of their ground.

Occasionally, however, your question, "How do you know?" may be countered with, "Do you know that it is not true?" And if you fluster and stammer, unable to respond successfully, it is possible that your opponent in the discussion will make the conclusion that *not knowing* it is *not* true, proves that it *is* true. This kind of conclusion makes the argument a fallacy.

Building a case on what is not known is a common technique of fiction writers. For example, a good science fiction story uses a great deal of information about which we are certain, to back up a theory about which we know nothing. The author might give the available evidence about life-supporting atmosphere on Mars and use it as evidence that life does exist on Mars. This is fine for

fiction, but sometimes the public mistakes fiction for fact. In the last twenty years, there have been many reports from individuals who have claimed to have seen flying saucers. Evidence for the existence of flying saucers is based on personal experience. (Such evidence is unacceptable to science because it is not verifiable.) When someone's belief in flying saucers is challenged by a person who does not believe in them, the believer replies, "No one has yet proved that they don't exist."

I Have My Troubles

The system of giving marks in school has many unfortunate side effects. By the time you are in secondary school, examination marks on a subject may make your heart beat faster. At times, you may feel the marking is unfair and you may want to discuss it with your teacher. This, of course, is your right, and most teachers want to know if they have made a mistake.

But in discussing the marks with your teacher, it is easy to fall into the fallacy of arguing from self-pity. You could tell her how unhappy your parents will be if she doesn't change the marks, how you won't be able to watch television for a week, and how a higher figure will get you the dog you have been wanting.

Put yourself in the teacher's place for a moment. If you were a teacher, and a student said those things to you, do you think you would change the marks? Doesn't it seem obvious that being allowed to watch television or getting a dog in the future has nothing to do with past class performance on which your teacher based your figures? Arguing from self-pity is another form of the fallacy of the unrelated conclusion.

Sometimes an argument based on pity can take a humorous twist. A lawyer once asked the jury not to punish his client too severely for murdering his mother and father because the client had become an "unfortunate orphan."

Appealing to Emotions

Every society has a system of values. That is, there are certain things that generally everyone agrees are desirable, and there are other things that most people consider undesirable. In our society, for example, most of us approve of freedom, love, youth, beauty, health, financial success, and democracy. Most of us do not like crime, poverty, ignorance, filth, corruption, and communism. These values are sometimes used to convince the public of many different arguments in areas that may not be related to the values at all.

Today, one of the most common sources for arguments that play on the emotions of the audience is in television commercials. People who smoke are usually young, good-looking, and are doing things we envy and admire. (Are the smokers you know like this?) One liquid detergent, it is claimed, can make hands "look

young again." (And everyone wants to look young. . . .) Social disaster can be traced to the failure to use a particular brand of hair cream or toothpaste. (When, in fact, any will do the job, if there is a job to be done.) Success is assured if you eat a certain cereal, cook with a certain oil, and drink a certain beer. All these ads have the same theme: Buy our product if you approve of, and want, youth, success, or fun. These products are being sold on the emotional appeal of ideals of our society, when, in fact, they have little, if anything, to do with these ideals.

Another example of trying to convince people by using their emotions is found in political speeches. Politicians often try to win the sentiments of a crowd by using "loaded" words to arouse emotions. These words have come to have special meanings. Politicians will speak passionately of "our great nation" and "our dear mothers" and "freedom for all." They will speak violently against "those Communists" and "crime in the streets." Often, the real meanings of their arguments are lost in the feelings brought out by these words.

Listen to the Expert

You could not even begin to count the times that some authority is quoted to make an argument convincing. Even in your own home your parents probably say things like, "Your Aunt Mary always said . . ." or "According to Dr. Henderson . . ." In turn, you may tell your parents things like "Beth's parents told her" or "My biology teacher says it's a good thing."

Quoting an authority is legitimate when the authority is an expert on the matter you are discussing. The opinions of professional tennis players, for example, give added weight to a discussion involving some fine point of the sport. The opinions of established book, film, and theatre critics have a great influence on public acceptance of new works.

Too often, however, an expert in one area is called upon to make a judgment in another. Film stars and sports heroes tell

us, for example, what bread to buy, what cereal to eat, and what hair tonic to use. Great scientists have been quoted for their views on religion, politics, ethics, and other topics where they are no more authorities than many other people.

When you hear people being quoted, you might ask yourself, "Are they experts on the matter we are considering?" If they are authorities, then the argument can be more convincing if they are quoted.

(25)

D

The Superstitious Fallacy

There are several fallacies that incorrectly consider one event to be the cause of another event. These fallacies are sometimes called fallacies of *false cause. The superstitious fallacy* is one example of a false-cause fallacy. In this case, a first event is considered the cause of a second event only *because it happened first.* You can imagine how a sequence of events could lead someone to the conclusion that "handling toads causes warts" or "walking under a ladder brings bad luck." Perhaps someone who developed warts remembered a time when he had handled a toad that looked as though it had warts. (Can you think of a way to disprove this conclusion?)

(26)

Sometimes this form of argument is used by politicians and editorial writers in newspapers. The party out of power blames the party in office for all wars, national disasters, or errors made during the time it was in office. The party in office assumes responsibility for favourable events that occurred during its administration. President Hoover, for example, was personally blamed for the Great Depression of the 1930's, although the economic weaknesses that were the real cause had developed long before he took office. People often simplify matters in a complicated situation by saying that it was caused by some event that took place or some person that happened to be around at that time.

The Naming Fallacy

The naming fallacy is also a kind of false-cause fallacy. In this case, no cause is actually given. The name that has been given to describe an event is used as the cause of the event. This fallacy is found in the conclusion, *John plays the violin well because he is talented.* "Talent" is the word that is supposed to be the cause of John's playing well. Yet, the only way we know that John is talented is because we hear him playing well. We are, in reality, saying "John plays well because he plays well." This is *the fallacy of circular reasoning.*

Two other words that are often used in naming fallacies are "ability" and "habit." They both refer to some description of behaviour. When someone has "ability" it means that whatever he is doing, he is doing it well. "Habit" is a word that describes behaviour that is so familiar we no longer have to think about doing it. Have you ever heard these words used as the cause for behaviour — *Sammy swims well because he has more swimming ability?* Or, *Bob can't stop biting his nails because it is such a habit?* (How do we know about Sammy's ability or Bob's habit?) The main danger with this fallacy is fooling ourselves into thinking that we have found a cause or reason for an event when actually we have not.

Deduction

The purpose of the premises of every argument is to give evidence that the conclusion is true. Logicians divide arguments into two types: *deductive* and *inductive*. The premises of a correct deductive argument contain *all* the evidence needed to prove the truth of a conclusion. This means that if the premises are true, the conclusion *must also* be true.

When logicians study deductive arguments, they decide whether the argument is valid or invalid rather than correct or incorrect. The words *valid* and *invalid* are technical terms. That is, they apply only to deductive arguments and are used to describe the relationship between premises and conclusion as follows: According to the rules of logic, a valid argument is one in which if the premises are true then the conclusion must also be true. In an invalid argument, it is possible to have true premises and a false conclusion.

(31)

As we have said, a logician is not interested in whether or not the premises are actually true. This is because sometimes it is not possible to know the truth of the premises, and any system that judges arguments has to be able to work even when truth is not known.

Valid arguments may have several forms. They may have one or more false premises and a true conclusion, they may have false premises and a false conclusion, and they may have true premises and a true conclusion. An argument is *always* invalid when it has true premises and a false conclusion.

Let us look at some examples. Here is a valid argument with true premises and a true conclusion:

All birds have feathers.   (true)
All chickens are birds.   (true)

Therefore, all chickens have feathers.   (true)

Here is a valid argument where the premises are false but the conclusion is true:

All mammals are fish.   (false)
All fish are warm-blooded.   (false)

All mammals are warm-blooded.   (true)

Here is a valid argument with false premises and a false conclusion:

(32)

All babies can read.   (false)
All readers are professors.   (false)

All babies are professors.   (false)

Here is an invalid argument. It contains true premises and a false conclusion:

All fish are animals.   (true)
All insects are animals.   (true)

All fish are insects.   (false)

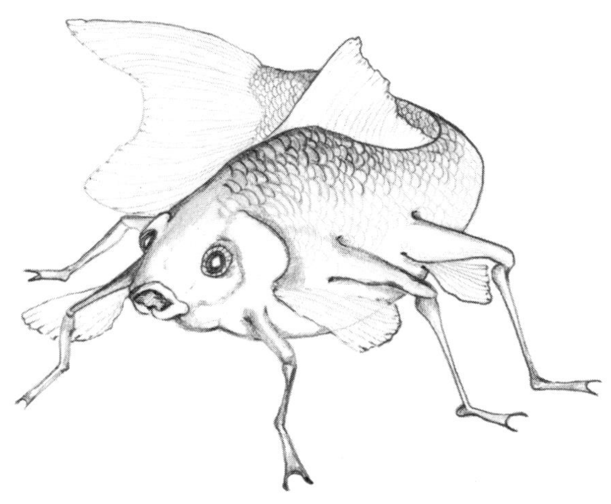

In the fallacies we discussed earlier, it is fairly easy to see how the conclusions do not follow from the premises. But many deductive arguments do not contain any of these fallacies and are still invalid arguments. These arguments contain errors in reasoning that are much more difficult to discover. It is the business of logic to set up a system by which arguments can be judged valid or invalid regardless of the actual truth or falsehood of the premises.

The Problem of Language

Without language, there would be no such thing as argument. However, language complicates the job of someone who is trying to see if a conclusion follows from premises. There are so many ways to say a sentence that gives the same information. Think, for instance, of all the ways you could give the information, "All sixth formers are students."

> Every sixth former is a student.
> Any sixth former is a student.
> Sixth formers are students.
> If anyone is a sixth former, he is a student.
> Anyone who is a sixth former is a student.
> All people that are not students are not sixth formers.
> A person is a sixth former only if he is a student.

(35)

Clearly, the first step in analyzing any argument is to simplify the language of the premises and conclusion into some standard type of statement. If all statements are said the same way, then this will reduce some of the confusion due to language itself.

Aristotle, the Greek philosopher who was the founder of logic, decided that he would first study arguments containing statements about classes or sets of objects. A set may be defined as a group of objects that has certain characteristics in common. So far, we have mentioned such sets as sixth formers, students, babies, professors, fish, insects, animals with feathers, etc. Statements containing sets are called *categorical* statements because they concern sets or categories of objects.

Categorical statements may take four different forms:

> All men are poets.
> No men are poets.
> Some men are poets.
> Some men are not poets.

Although categorical statements are not found in every deductive argument, they are important enough to be considered one of the main types of statement. They form the basis for the system from which modern logic has grown. We can only begin to understand complicated arguments when we have mastered simple ones.

Syllogisms

Before we begin it might be a good idea to get pencil and paper to write out answers to the questions that will be asked in the examples. We will be considering in our study of logic one aspect that is very disciplined and clear-cut. It is not difficult to understand, but you will have more fun if you are able to work out the answers yourself. Proving arguments are valid or invalid is as much fun as any crossword puzzle, and when you understand how to do this, you can make up your own examples.

A syllogism is an argument with a very simple form. Its simplicity makes it easier to decide whether or not it is valid. In order for an argument to be a syllogism, it must have the following characteristics: 1) All the statements are categorical statements. 2) There are two premises and a conclusion. 3) The two premises and conclusion together contain three different categories or sets. Each set appears in two of the three statements.

We have already included some syllogisms that are made up of only one kind of categorical statement. Here are some other examples. See if you can name the sets in each example:

Some people who eat butter have heart disease.
No person with heart disease can climb trees.

Some people who eat butter cannot climb trees.

All ducks waddle.
Nothing that waddles is graceful.

No ducks are graceful.

Some bald people wear wigs.
None of your friends wear wigs.

Some bald people are not your friends.

Once an argument is stated as a syllogism, the form of the syllogism can be seen clearly if letters are used to represent the different sets. It is common to let the letter *S* represent the *subject term* in a conclusion and let the letter *P* represent the *final* (or *predicate*) *term* in a conclusion. The *middle term*, found in both premises, is represented by the letter *M*. With this system, all conclusions would be one of the following statements:

All *S* is *P*.
No *S* is *P*.
Some *S* is *P*.
Some *S* is not *P*.

Now let's look at an actual syllogism:

All silly people make jokes.
Some silly people are children.

Some children make jokes.

S (subject term of the conclusion) represents *children*. *P* represents *people who make jokes*. The middle term M stands for *silly people*. The form of this syllogism becomes:

All *M* is *P*.
Some *M* is *S*.

Some *S* is *P*.

See if you can write out the form of the following syllogisms:

All tennis players are conceited.
Some tennis players are rich.

Some conceited people are rich.

All people who sleep past 6 A.M. are lazy.
No lazy people are movie stars.

No movie stars sleep past 6 A.M.

The errors of reasoning in syllogisms are directly related to the form of a syllogism. Some syllogisms are clearly invalid on inspection. That is, they contain premises known to be true and a conclusion that is known to be false. For example:

All roses smell sweet.   (true)
Some sweet-smelling flowers are honeysuckle.   (true)

Some roses are honeysuckle.   (false)

One of the rules of logic is that any syllogism with a proven invalid form such as the example above, is always considered invalid, even if it seems to make sense and the premises and conclusion are all true statements. The following example has the same form as the invalid example just given. It, too, is invalid:

All roses smell sweet.
Some sweet-smelling flowers have thorns.

Some roses have thorns.

(41)

E*

Testing for Validity

One way to see if a syllogism is valid or invalid is to see if you can construct an argument with the same exact form but with true premises and a false conclusion. Look at the following example. Can you be certain about the truth or falsehood of any of the statements?

> No democrats believe in dictatorships.
> All people who believe in dictatorships are ruthless.
> ____
>
> No democrats are ruthless.

The first step in finding out if the above example is valid is to state its form with the symbols *S*, *P*, and *M*. This argument has the form:

> No *S* is *M*.   *S* stands for democrats.
> All *M* is *P*.   *M* stands for people who believe in dictatorships.
> ——————
> No S is P.   *P* stands for ruthless people.

We can construct the following argument with the same form that proves any argument with this form is invalid:

> No bread is cake.   (true)   *S* stands for bread.
> All cake is made with flour.   (true)   *M* stands for cake.
> ——————————————
> No bread is made with flour. (false)   *P* stands for flour.

This method of testing for validity is quite inconvenient. It is sometimes difficult to dream up an argument with true premises and a false conclusion, and you cannot be sure that just because *you* can't prove that it is invalid means that it is valid. Many logicians have tried to discover better ways to see if arguments are valid. They have used systems of symbols and diagrams. But the easiest and most foolproof method was invented by John Venn.

Venn employed diagrams with overlapping circles to represent the sets in categorical statements. Suppose we wanted to diagram the statement "All bees are insects." We would draw two overlapping circles, and let the circle on the left represent the set of bees and the circle on the right represent the set of insects.

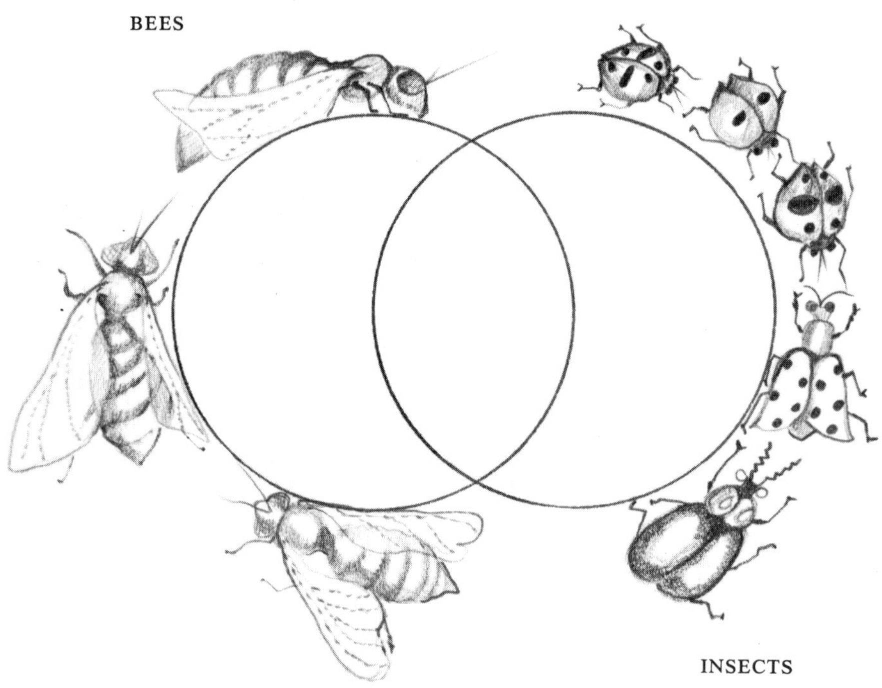

The statement "All bees are insects" means that there is no member of the bee set that is not in the set of insects. This is shown in the diagram by shading out all of the circle representing bees that does not overlap the circle representing insects.

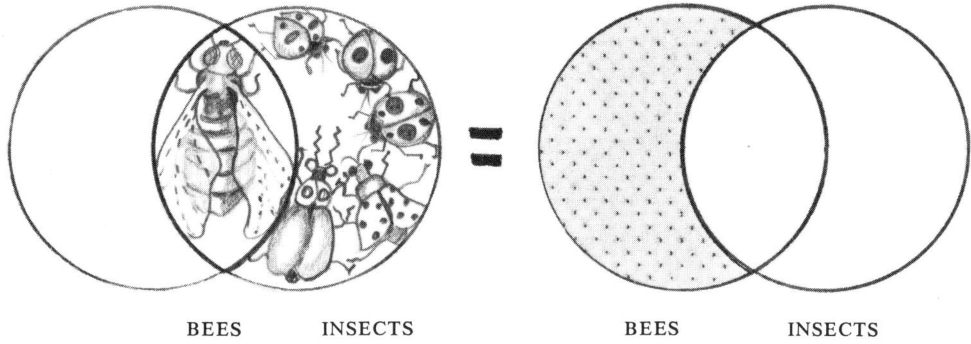

BEES   INSECTS   BEES   INSECTS

Any categorical statement of the form "All *S* is *P*" is diagrammed in this manner:

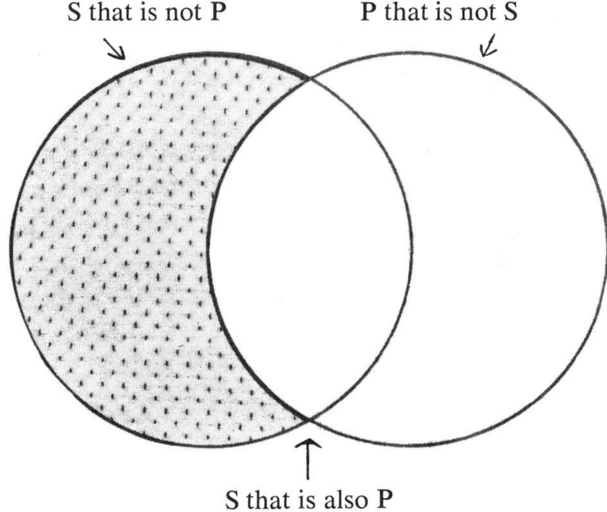

The statement "No *S* is *P*" means that the set of objects that includes both *S* and *P* does not exist. It is diagrammed by shading out the overlap between the two circles:

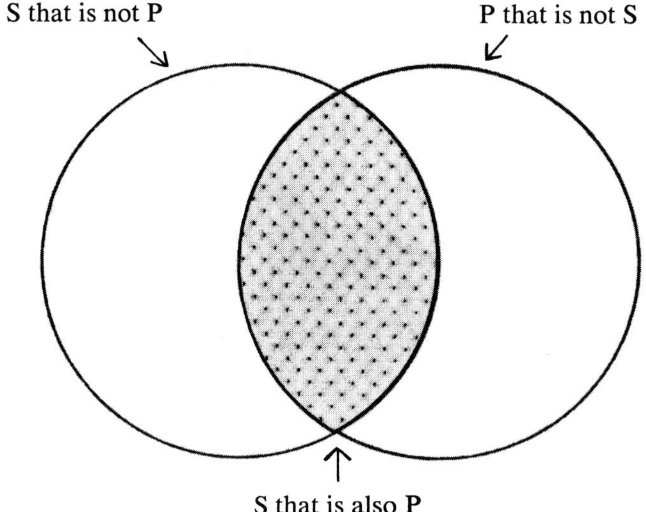

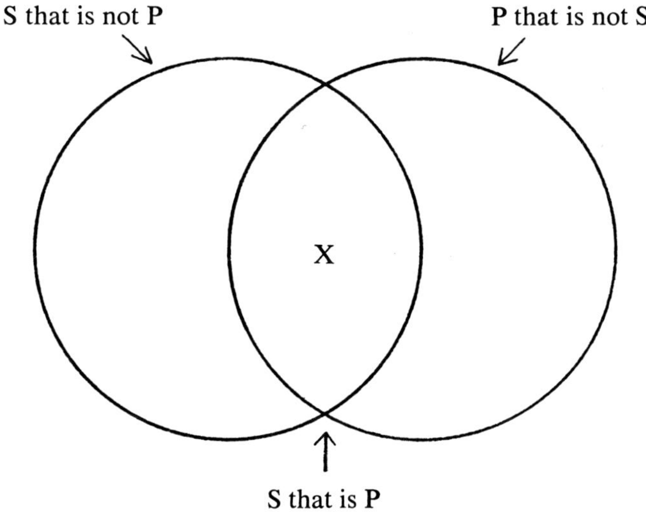

The statement "Some *S* is *P*" means that there is at least one member of set *S* that is in set *P*. This is diagrammed by putting an *x* (representing that one case) in the overlapping part of the diagram:

(47)

The statement "Some S is not P" means that there is at least one member of set S that is not included in set P. This is diagrammed by putting an x in the part of the S circle that does not overlap the P circle:

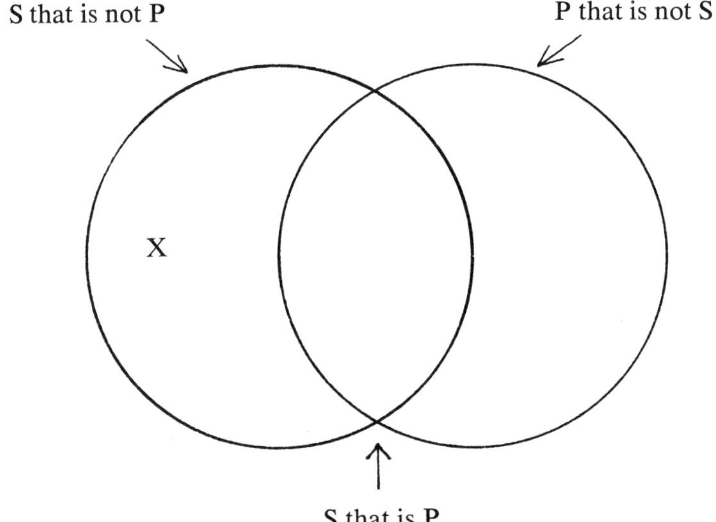

In order to prove the validity of a syllogism, three overlapping circles are used. Each circle is labelled for one of the sets in the syllogism:

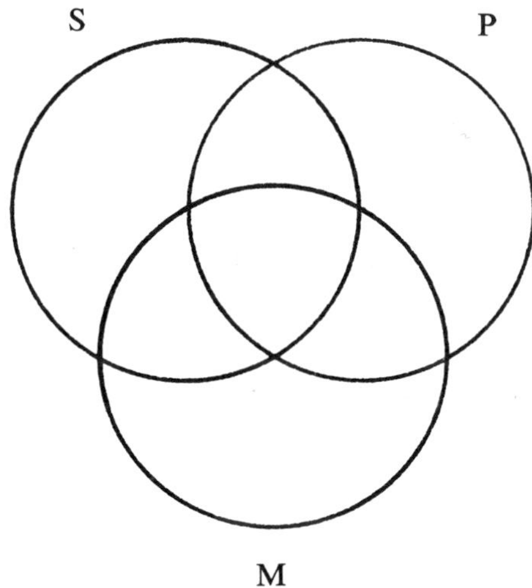

When a Venn diagram is used to test a syllogism for validity, each premise is diagrammed by looking only at the two circles representing the sets in each premise. Let us diagram a syllogism with the form:

All S is M.
All M is P.

All S is P.

(49)

First, we diagram the premise "All S is M" by shading in all of the S circle that is not in the M circle:

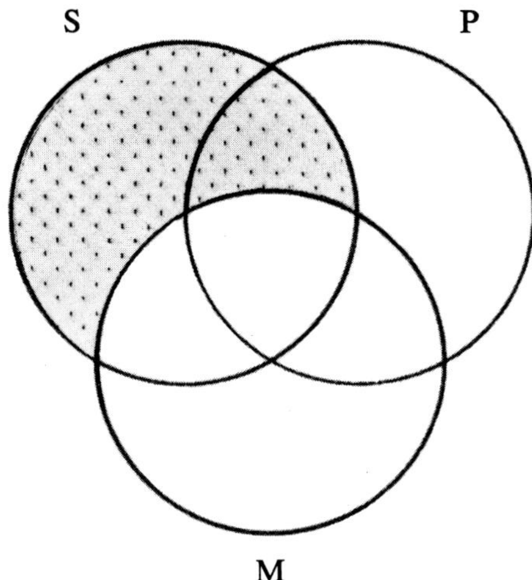

Next, we diagram the premise "All M is P" by shading in all of the M circle that is not in the P circle:

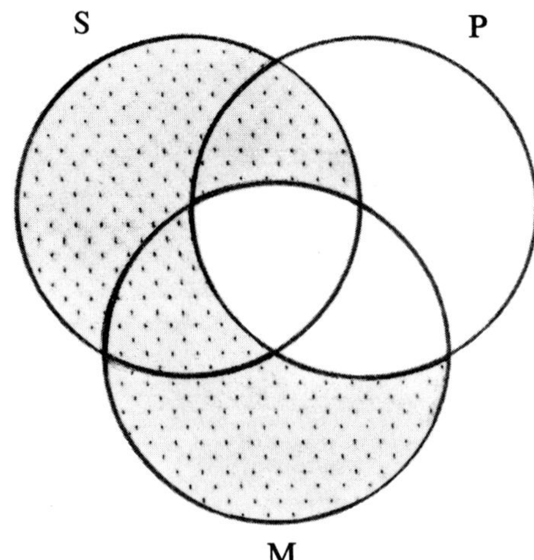

If the syllogism is valid, the conclusion "All *S* is *P*" is automatically diagrammed. That is, all of the *S* circle that is not in the *P* circle is shaded in the process of diagramming the two premises. As you can see, all of the *S* circle that is not in the *P* circle is shaded, and the syllogism is proven valid. (Disregard that part of the *S* circle in the P circle that is shaded.)

In the following syllogism, one of the premises begins with the word "some." This premise should be diagrammed after a premise that begins with "all" or "no."

All eagles can fly.
Some pigs cannot fly.
———————————————
Some pigs are not eagles.

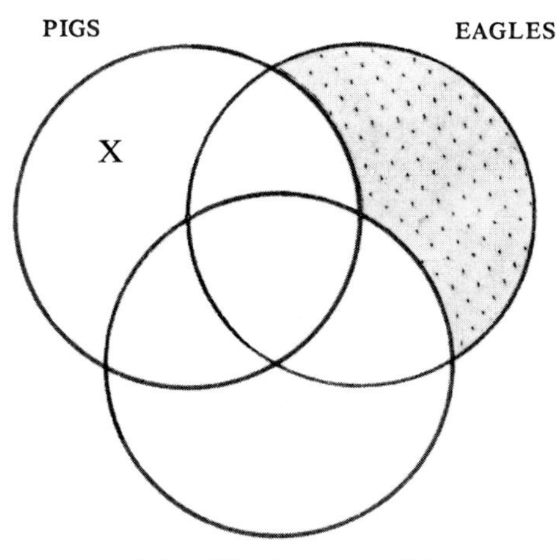

This argument is valid because the x appears in the part of the pig circle that means there is at least one pig that is not an eagle.

Here is an example of an invalid syllogism that includes a premise beginning with the word "some":

No frogs are poets.
Some ducks are not poets.
____

Some ducks are not frogs.

We first diagram " No frogs are poets":

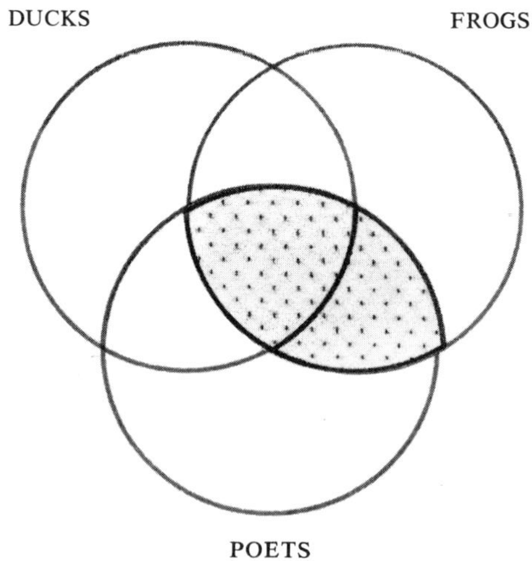

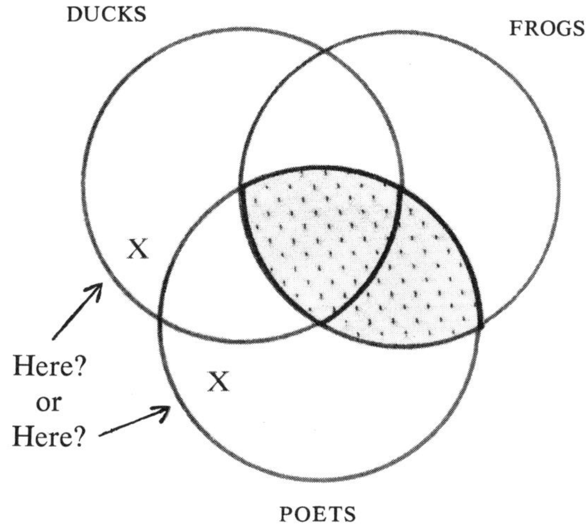

Now the question is, Where do we put the x that indicates there is at least one duck that is not a poet?

(53)

We cannot put the x in either place because if we did, we would be saying more about ducks that are not poets than we know from the premises. This uncertainty about where to put the x is enough to make the syllogism invalid.

See if you can diagram the following syllogisms. These and many others in the book were written by Lewis Carroll, author of *Alice in Wonderland*. They come from his textbook on logic:

All who are anxious to learn work hard.
Some of these boys work hard.

Some of these boys are anxious to learn.

All lions are fierce.
Some lions do not drink coffee.

Some creatures that drink coffee are not fierce.

No professors are ignorant.
All ignorant people are vain.

No professors are vain.

No emperors are dentists.
All dentists are dreaded by children.

No emperors are dreaded by children.

No monkeys are soldiers.
All monkeys are mischievous.

Some mischievous creatures are not soldiers.

Some creatures that drink coffee are not fierce.

Induction

Induction is a form of reasoning that is very different from deduction. But like deduction, inductive arguments consist of premises that support conclusions. One basic difference between induction and deduction is that a correct inductive argument may have true premises and a false conclusion. This is because inductive arguments do not *prove* that conclusions are true. At best, the premises only establish that a conclusion is likely or probable. The premises serve as some (but not all) of the evidence needed for a conclusion, because the premises contain less information than the information that is stated in the conclusion. As a result, inductive arguments are not judged as *valid* or *invalid*. (These terms apply only to deductive arguments.) Inductive arguments are judged as more or less probable. A strong inductive argument is highly probable and a weak inductive argument is considered improbable.

Induction plays an important part in everyday life. Every housewife uses inductive reasoning, for example, when she does her shopping. Did you ever watch your mother select tomatoes? She picks up a tomato, examines it, squeezes it, and then either accepts it or rejects it. She may be reasoning: "Good-tasting to-

matoes that we have eaten in the past have been firm, unblemished, and red. Therefore, there is a good chance that a tomato that is firm, unblemished, and red will taste good." Now it is possible that a tomato that has these qualities may not taste good. It could, for example, be rotten inside. Yet the argument that a tomato with these characteristics will also be good tasting is a strong, probable argument.

The conclusion of an inductive argument is a general statement based on premises about specific examples. The conclusion about the characteristics of tomatoes that may be a clue to their taste is based on the experience of selecting and eating many tomatoes. This form of inductive reasoning is based on the sampling of many individual cases. The argument becomes stronger as the number of individual cases increases.

Induction by Analogy

Many inductive arguments base conclusions on similar situations where the conclusion is known. An example of such an argument is found in the writing of Herbert Spencer, who lived during the time of the great Industrial Revolution when fortunes were made very easily. He liked to compare this society to laws of nature discovered by Charles Darwin. Spencer felt that in his industrial society the most successful people were the result of the same kind of forces that operated on organisms in nature. There was a form of "natural selection" in the society in which "the fittest survived." He borrowed many examples for his social theory from the works of Charles Darwin. In fact, his philosophy was called Social Darwinism.

But there is a big trap in arguing by analogy. The comparison can be carried so far that it is possible to come to the wrong conclusion. This can be shown as follows: "He looks like his father; he is a good athlete like his father; he talks like his father; he will probably be a good lawyer like his father."

Induction in Science

Inductive reasoning is at the very core of the discovery of scientific truth. Scientists ask themselves questions (sometimes called hypotheses) that begin with these four words, "What would happen if . . .?" These questions are answered by experiments which give them information about these specific events. After many such experiments, scientists come to make a general statement that may be known as a scientific generalization or natural law. They could say, for example, "What would happen if I heat up this iron rod?" They heat it and find that it gets longer. Then other kinds of metal rods are heated. After many tests, they conclude, "Metals expand when heated."

Induction, in science, is used for determining truth. It has been very successful as judged by the progress of science. Establishing the truth of premises is extremely important in induction because

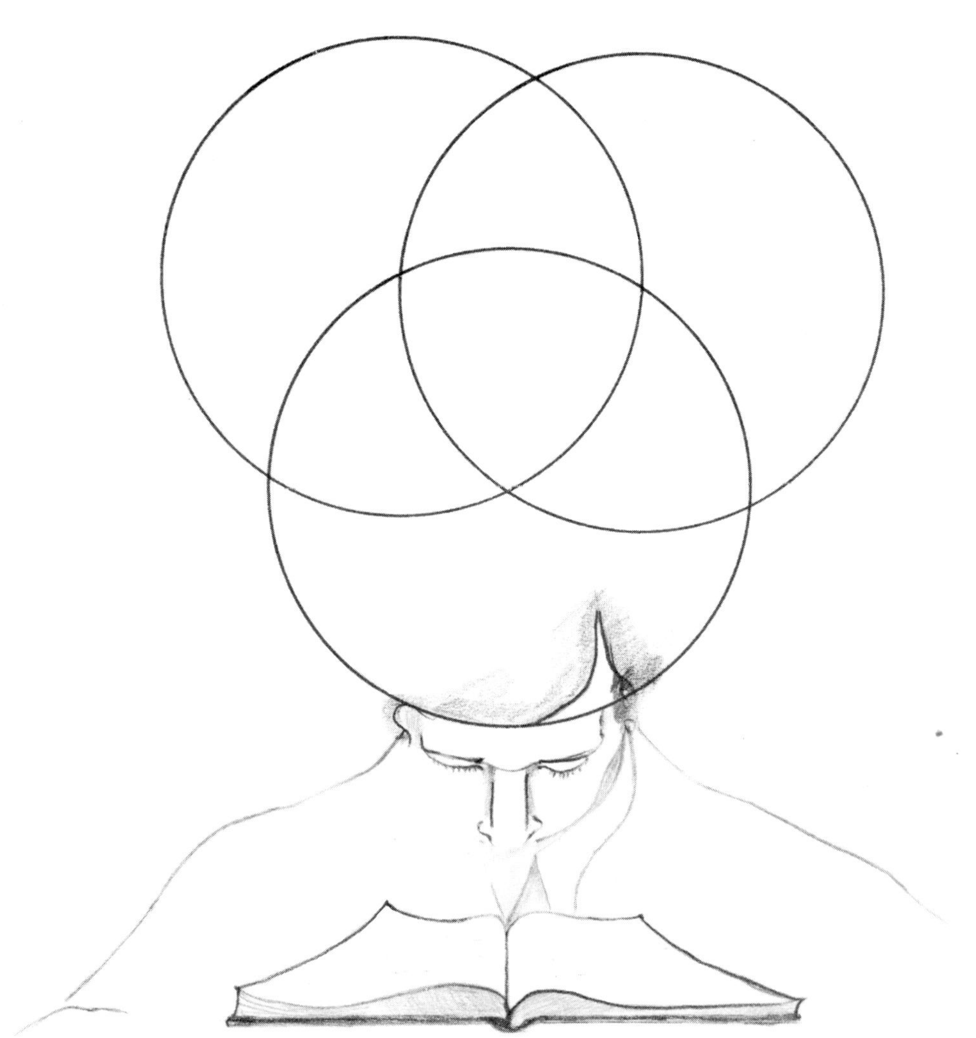

it is the truth of the premises that establishes the conclusion as more or less likely. Truths established by induction are later used as premises in deductive arguments. For example: Metals expand when heated. Gold is a metal. Gold expands when heated.

After studying these kinds of logical arguments, perhaps you are better able to answer certain questions for yourself when you read or hear an argument: Is this inductive or deductive reasoning? Are any of the ordinary fallacies being committed? Is this deductive argument valid? Is there enough evidence in this inductive argument to support the conclusion?

Index